CHECKERBOARD HOW-TO LIBRARY

COOL ART

Cool Calligraphy

THE ART OF CREATIVITY
FOR KIDS!

ANDERS HANSON

ABDO
Publishing Company

CONTENTS

Published by ABDO Publishing Company, 8000 West 78th Street, Edina, Minnesota 55439.

Copyright © 2009 by Abdo Consulting Group, Inc. International copyrights reserved in all countries.

No part of this book may be reproduced in any form without written permission from the publisher. Checkerboard Library™ is a trademark and logo of ABDO Publishing Company.

Printed in the United States.

Editor: Pam Price

Series Concept: Nancy Tuminelly

Cover and Interior Design: Anders Hanson, Mighty Media

Photo Credits: Anders Hanson, Shutterstock

Hanson, Anders, 1980-
  Cool calligraphy : the art of creativity for kids / Anders Hanson.
      p. cm. -- (Cool art)
  Includes index.
  ISBN 978-1-60453-145-9
  1. Lettering--Technique--Juvenile literature. 2. Calligraphy--Technique--Juvenile literature. I. Title.

NK3600.H26 2008
745.6'1--dc22
                                              2008019885

Get the Picture!

When a step number in an activity has a colored circle around it, look for the picture that goes with it. The picture's border will be the same color as the circle.

THE ART OF creativity

You Are Creative

Being creative is all about using your imagination to make new things. Coming up with new ideas and bringing them to life is part of being human. Everybody is creative! Creative thinking takes time and practice. But that's okay, because being creative is a lot of fun!

Calling All Artists

Maybe you believe that you aren't good at art. Maybe you have some skills that you want to improve. The purpose of this book is to help you develop your visual creativity. Remember that your artistic skills improve every time you make art. The activities in this book can help you become the creative artist you want to be!

Creativity Tips

- Stay positive.
- There is no wrong way to be creative.
- Allow yourself to make mistakes.
- Tracing isn't cheating.
- Practice, practice, practice.
- Be patient.
- Have fun!

Calligraphy is COOL!

The pen is mightier than the sword.
—Edward Bulwer-Lytton

What Is Calligraphy?

Calligraphy means "beautiful writing." It is the art of drawing letters and words by hand. There are many ways to make writing beautiful.

The Beautiful Word

The writing we use today is based on the Latin alphabet. The **Roman Empire** developed the Latin alphabet over 2,600 years ago. It's the most widely used alphabet in the world. Western calligraphy uses the Latin alphabet.

Western calligraphy has a rich history with many varied styles. This book will cover **italic** and **Gothic** scripts. They are **traditional** forms of Western calligraphy.

Many other cultures have rich traditions in calligraphy. The Chinese, Japanese, Hebrew, and Islamic cultures are just a few.

ITALIC SCRIPT *Aa Bb Cc Dd Ee*

GOTHIC SCRIPT **Aa Bb Cc Dd Ee**

CUNEIFORM WRITING

The Written Word

Written language first appeared over 5,000 years ago in Mesopotamia. At first, writing was simply a way to keep track of business. People pressed the end of a reed into a clay tablet to make wedge-shaped marks in it. These marks formed letters and words that described the agreement. This style of writing is called cuneiform.

Don't Be a Judge!

When discussing a work of art, avoid using the words listed below. They offer judgments without saying much about the character of the work.

- good
- right
- silly
- bad
- wrong
- stupid

Learn Calligraphy!

Learning calligraphy is fun! All you need to begin is paper and a pen.

Some of the **techniques** may seem difficult at first. You may not be satisfied with your first attempts. Just remember that great artists are not always satisfied with their work. Part of what makes great is that they are always trying to get better.

You don't need to be good at calligraphy now to become a great calligrapher. You just need the desire to learn and become better!

Have Patience

Be patient with yourself. Changes won't happen overnight. When you do some work that you don't like, don't throw it out. Save it so you can look back later and see how much you've improved! Have **confidence** in yourself. You can do anything you set your mind to!

PAGE FROM THE *BOOK OF KELLS* (AD 800)

The Book of Kells

The *Book of Kells* is one of the finest examples of Western calligraphy. It was created by Irish monks about 1,200 years ago. It contains the four gospels from the *New Testament* of the Bible. The text is written in Latin.

TOOLS OF THE TRADE

Each activity in this book has a list of the tools and materials you will need. When you come across a tool you don't know, turn back to this page. You can find most of these items at your local art store.

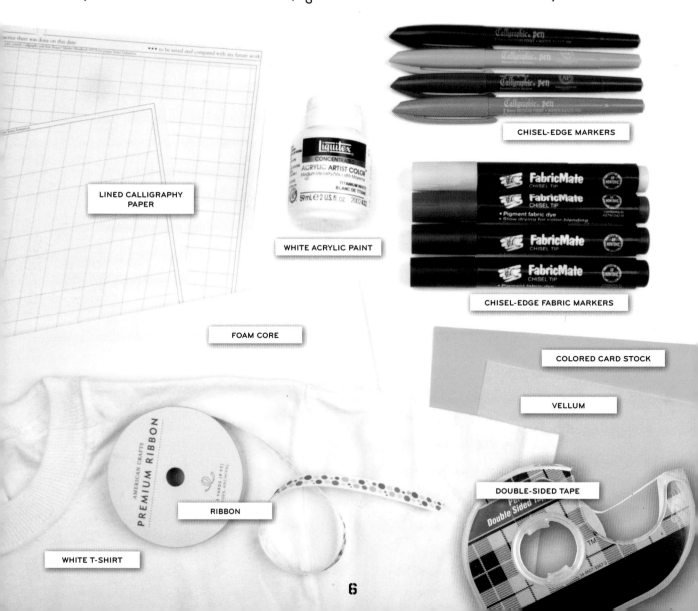

LINED CALLIGRAPHY PAPER

WHITE ACRYLIC PAINT

CHISEL-EDGE MARKERS

CHISEL-EDGE FABRIC MARKERS

FOAM CORE

COLORED CARD STOCK

VELLUM

RIBBON

DOUBLE-SIDED TAPE

WHITE T-SHIRT

6

Parts of a Letter

Lowercase letters have three parts. Here are some terms that will help you describe them.

Ascender

The ascender is the part of a letter that rises above the waistline. The letters *b, d, f, h, k, l,* and *t* have ascenders.

X-Height

The height of the lowercase letter *x* is called the x-height. The letters *a, c, e, m, n, o, r, s, u, v, w,* and *z* are usually the same height as the *x*.

Descender

A descender drops below the baseline. The letters *g, j, p, q,* and *y* have descenders. Sometimes *f* has a descender too.

WAISTLINE

The waistline marks the top of the x-height.

BASELINE

The baseline is the line that most letters rest on.

7

Strokes

This guide explains the marks that will show you the order and direction of the strokes.

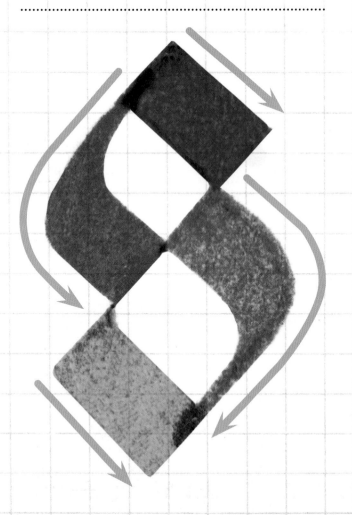

Stroke Order

Each letter is made up of one or more strokes. These strokes are drawn in a specific order.

 First stroke

 Second stroke

 Third stroke

 Fourth stroke

Stroke Direction

Arrows show you which direction a stroke should go. Start at the end of the arrow and finish at the tip of the arrow.

Entrance Stroke

An entrance stroke is a small stroke that leads into a stroke.

Exit Stroke

An exit stroke is a small stroke that finishes a stroke.

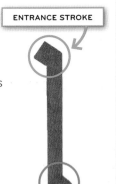

ENTRANCE STROKE

EXIT STROKE

Decorations

Decorations are features added to letters to change their appearance.

Swash

A swash is a long entrance or exit stroke. Swashes decorate many capital letters in **italic** script.

Double Stroke

A double stroke is a way to make letters more ornate. In a double stroke, two similar strokes replace a single stroke.

Beaks and Claws

Gothic capitals are often decorated with jagged strokes called beaks and claws. To add these, move your pen downward in short zigzag fashion over a **vertical** line.

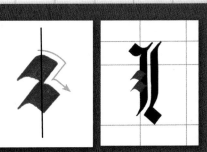

Techniques

Here are a few simple **techniques** to learn before you begin writing letters. Grab some paper and a calligraphy pen and try them out!

Positioning the Paper

Right-handers should tilt their paper so the right edge is slightly higher than the left edge. Left-handers should tilt their paper so the right edge is much lower than the left edge.

Right-handed position

Left-handed position

Writing With a Wide Nib

Calligraphy markers and pens usually have wide, flat **nibs**. This allows them to make both thick and thin lines. Always keep the entire width of the nib on the paper. You don't need to press very hard.

Incorrect

This stroke is uneven. The right side of the nib did not touch the paper.

Incorrect

This stroke is uneven. The left side of the nib did not touch the paper.

Correct!

This stroke is even. Both sides of the nib were touching the paper.

Diagonal Pen Position

Many styles of calligraphy call for a diagonal pen position. Choose a pen with a wide nib. Hold the pen so the nib is halfway between **vertical** and **horizontal**. Try to keep the pen at this angle as you write.

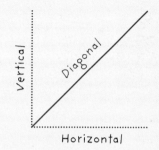

The italic **x** has two diagonal downstrokes.

The Gothic **m** has three downstrokes.

The italic **l** is a downstroke.

Downstrokes

Downstrokes are lines that go downward. They can be vertical, diagonal, or curved. To make a vertical downstroke, place your marker on the paper and draw a line straight down. To create a diagonal downstroke, move the pen right or left as you draw downward.

Upstrokes

Upstrokes are lines that go upward. They can be vertical, diagonal, or curved. To make a vertical upstroke, place your marker on the paper and draw a line straight up. To create a diagonal upstroke, move the pen right or left as you draw upward.

The Gothic **g** has an upstroke.

The italic **p** has an upstroke.

FUNKY Frame

Practice your pen position while making beautiful borders!

Hold Steady!

When writing calligraphy, always hold your marker in the same position. That way your letters will look even. In this project, you'll practice the diagonal pen position. This position is also used in **italic** and **Gothic** calligraphy.

Stuff You'll Need

Flat picture frame or foam core, white paint, chisel-edge color markers, paper or lined calligraphy pad

1. Find a flat picture frame or have an adult cut one out of foam core or cardboard. Paint it white and allow it to dry in a safe place.

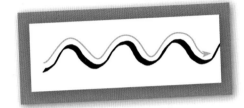

2. Let's practice! On a piece of paper, draw a large zigzag going from left to right. Start by drawing a thin diagonal upstroke. Then draw a thick diagonal downstroke. Repeat these strokes several times. Don't lift your marker off the paper between strokes.

3. Now try a wavy line. Make it the same height as the zigzag. Draw each wave to look the same.

4. Finally, try a much smaller zigzag. It should be so small that it's hard to see the thin upstrokes. This zigzag should look like a string of diamonds.

5. Now get out your frame. Using a colored marker, draw a large zigzag on each side of the frame.

6. Choose a different-colored marker. Draw a wavy line on top of the zigzag.

7. Decorate the remaining space with the small zigzag pattern from step 4.

Lowercase ITALIC

This slanted script is easy to learn!

the quick

brown fox

jumps over

a lazy dog

The Italic Slant

Italic script is written at a slight slant. For some writers, using a slant feels natural. For others, it may take some time to master. If you're having trouble, you may want to buy lined calligraphy paper. Make sure it has a slanted grid for italic script.

Pen Position
Diagonal

Stuff You'll Need
Chisel-edge marker, paper or lined calligraphy pad

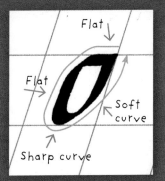

The a-shape (a, c, d, g, q, u, and y)

The main shape of the **a** is used in other letters too. It's a fairly tricky shape. But it takes only one stroke. It has a flat top and a sharply curved bottom.

The second stroke of the **d** has both an entrance and an exit stroke.

a c d g q u y

The **a** has an exit stroke.

The b-shape (b, h, k, m, n, p, and r)

Another common shape is the lower part of the **b**. It looks like an a-shape that's been turned on its head! It has a sharply curved top and a flat bottom.

b h k m n p r

The **m** is a little wider than the other letters.

The **h** is the same as the **b**, except it has an open bottom.

Try to make the **m** with one stroke.

The **p** is done in two strokes.

Straight Lines (f, i, j, l, and t)

Some letters are made mostly of straight lines. Remember to draw them at the same slant.

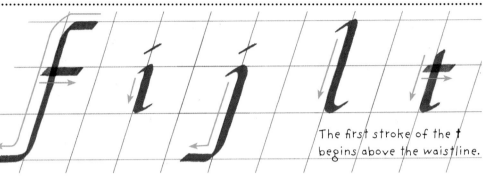

The first stroke of the *t* begins above the waistline.

e and o

These letters are all curves!

v and w

Draw the final upstroke with a little curve.

s, x, and z

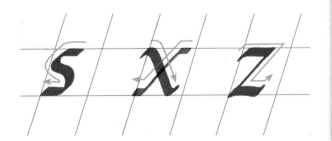

Letter Spacing

When letters form a word, the space between the letters is important. Too much or too little space between the letters makes words hard to read. The sentence on the first page of each calligraphy style shows how to correctly space the letters in that style.

These graceful capitals are really fun to write!

Size and Slant

Uppercase **italic** letters are slanted just like the lowercase letters. The height of the uppercase letters is halfway between the waistline and the tops of the ascenders.

Pen Position
Diagonal

Stuff You'll Need
Chisel-edge marker, paper or lined calligraphy pad

The Quick

Brown Fox

Jumps Over

a Lazy Dog

The Basic Strokes

The two basic strokes are the downstroke and the swash. Once you master these strokes, learning the others will be easy!

The Downstroke The Swash

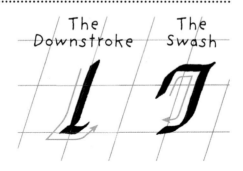

C, G, O, and Q

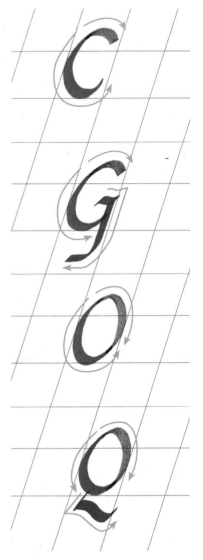

F, P, R, and T

The second stroke of these letters begins like the swash stroke.

B, D, E, and I

The first stroke of the *D* and the *E* has a much longer exit stroke.

⌐ The *B* has a medium-length exit stroke.

18

H, K, N, and U

The second stroke of the **H** is just like the letter **I**.

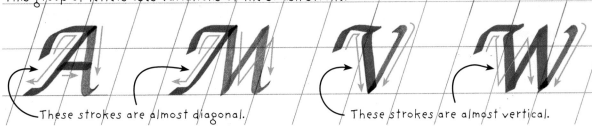

The end of the first stroke of the **U** curves up and to the right.

A, M, V, and W

This group of letters uses variations of the swash stroke.

These strokes are almost diagonal.

These strokes are almost vertical.

J, L, S, X, Y, and Z

These letters do not use the basic strokes.

Lowercase GOTHIC

Get **medieval** with these fancy letters!

the quick
brown fox
jumps over
a lazy dog

Blackletter

Lowercase **Gothic** writing is often called blackletter. This is because the letters have thick black strokes placed closely together. When the letters fill a page, it becomes almost black!

Gothic script was popular from the 12th to 14th centuries. The term *Gothic* was given to the script in the 15th century. At the time, *Gothic* meant "crude" or "tasteless."

Pen Position
Diagonal

Stuff You'll Need
Chisel-edge marker, paper or lined calligraphy pad

The Basic Strokes

There are two basic strokes for making lowercase Gothic letters. One is short, the other is tall. They each have an entrance stroke and an exit stroke. Practice these strokes until you're comfortable with them. Then try making some letters.

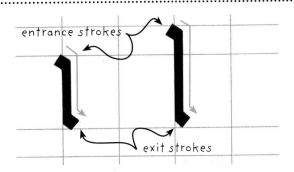

entrance strokes

exit strokes

i, m, n, r, and x

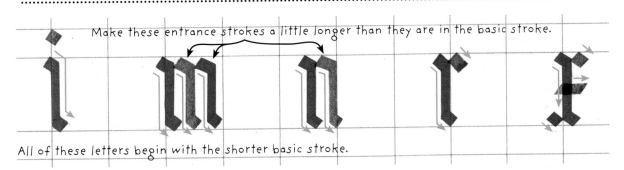

Make these entrance strokes a little longer than they are in the basic stroke.

All of these letters begin with the shorter basic stroke.

d and e

The first stroke of these letters has a slightly longer exit stroke.

f and t

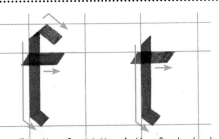

For the *f* and the *t*, the first stroke begins above the waistline.

u, v, and w

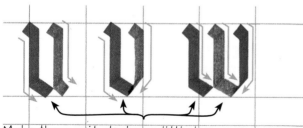

Make these exit strokes a little longer than in the basic stroke.

b, h, k, and l

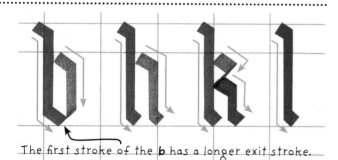

The first stroke of the **b** has a longer exit stroke.

a, c, o, and q

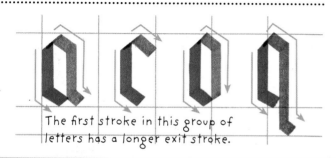

The first stroke in this group of letters has a longer exit stroke.

j and p

For the **j** and the **p**, the first stroke ends below the baseline.

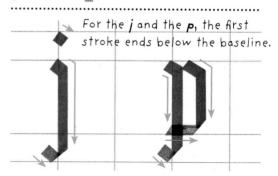

g and y

Make a longer exit stroke on the first stroke when writing **g** and **y**.

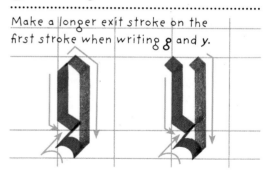

s and z

The **s** is made in four stokes.

22

UPPERCASE GOTHIC

These big capital letters make bold statements!

Use Sparingly!

Use these capital letters to begin words. A whole word written in uppercase **Gothic** may be hard to read.

The Quick Brown Fox Jumps Over a Lazy Dog

Pen Position
Diagonal

Stuff You'll Need
Chisel-edge marker, paper or lined calligraphy pad

Basic Strokes

There are two sets of basic strokes for making uppercase **Gothic** letters. All Gothic capitals use one of these strokes, except the letters S, X, and Z. Try these strokes before you go on to making the letters.

For the rest of this project, these basic strokes will be shown in magenta only. Return to this section if you have trouble remembering the individual strokes.

The Double Stroke

The Curve

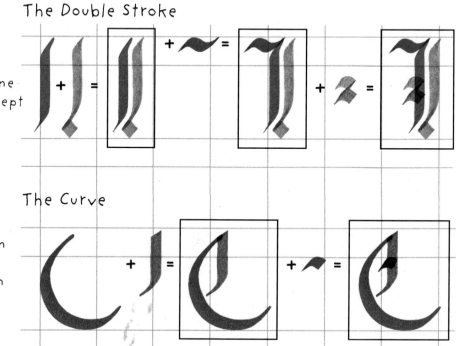

A, M, N, and T

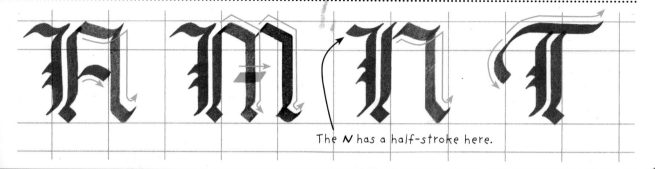

The **N** has a half-stroke here.

C, G, O, and Q

B, D, P, and R

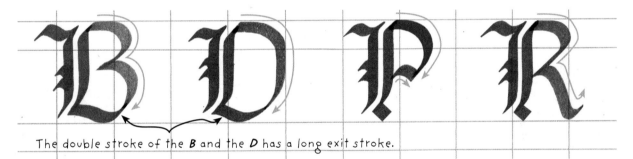

The double stroke of the *B* and the *D* has a long exit stroke.

E, F, H, and K

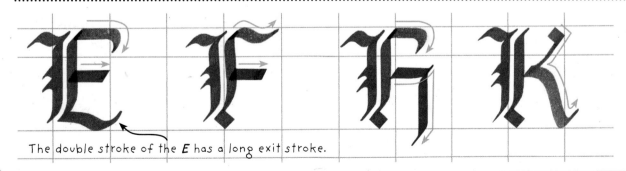

The double stroke of the *E* has a long exit stroke.

U, V, W, and Y

The **V** is the only letter from this group to use a full stroke here.

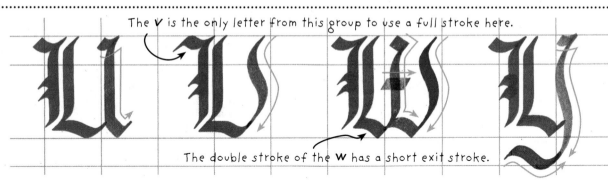

The double stroke of the **W** has a short exit stroke.

I, J, and L

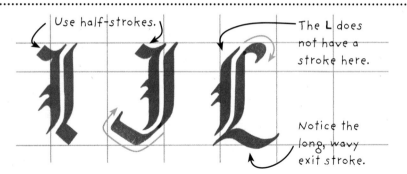

Use half-strokes.

The **L** does not have a stroke here.

Notice the long, wavy exit stroke.

S, X and Z

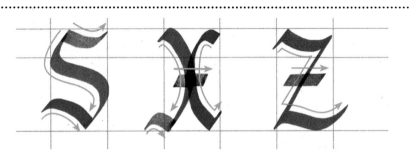

Decorate Your Letters!

You can write uppercase **Gothic** letters with single strokes or double strokes. The examples shown here have double strokes.

Feel free to add more beaks and claws to your letters. But don't add too many. If you do, you might not be able to tell what letter it is!

CALLIGRAPHY *Card*

Make a beautiful invitation for your next party!

1 Cut a piece of colored card stock to measure 6 inches (15.2 cm) by 8 inches (20.3 cm).

2 Cut a piece of vellum to measure 5.5 inches (14 cm) by 7.5 inches (19 cm).

3 Place the vellum on top of the card stock. Punch two holes at the top using a hole punch. Make them about 2 inches (5 cm) apart.

4 Thread the ribbon through the holes. Tie a bow on the front of the card.

5 Write a short invitation in your favorite style of calligraphy! Hint: place a sheet of lined calligraphy paper under the vellum to guide you as you write. Add a border around the invitation if you'd like!

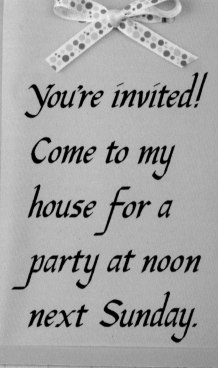

You're invited! Come to my house for a party at noon next Sunday.

Stuff You'll Need

Colored card stock, vellum, ruler, scissors, hole punch, ribbon, lined calligraphy paper, chisel-edge marker

LETTERS *T-Shirt*

Show off your lettering skills with a funky, colorful T-shirt!

Stuff You'll Need

Cardboard, double-sided tape or adhesive paper, blank white T-shirt, chisel-edge fabric markers

1. Cut a piece of cardboard to fit inside the T-shirt. It should fill most of the shirt.

2. Apply double-sided tape or adhesive paper to one side of the cardboard. Adhesive paper works better than tape.

3. Put the piece of cardboard inside the T-shirt. Press the front of the shirt against the sticky side of the cardboard. The cardboard will give you a better surface to write on. It will also keep the ink from bleeding through the shirt.

4. Decide what you want to write on your shirt. You could write your name or the name of your favorite band or sports team. Or you could just write some of your favorite letters.

5. Get out the colored fabric markers.

6. Begin writing your letters or words on the T-shirt. You could write in one style of calligraphy. Or you could write in a few different styles!

7. Read the instructions on the fabric markers to learn how to care for your new shirt.

Writing on Fabric

Writing on fabric is more difficult than writing on paper. It's hard to get fabric to stay in one place. Every time you make a stroke, the marker stretches the fabric.

Try not to press too hard. Draw each line with many short strokes instead of one long one. This will help you write beautiful letters on fabric.

what's next?

Taking Care of Your Calligraphy

Storing or treating calligraphy projects improperly can wreck them. Here are a few tips to help keep your calligraphy in good condition.

If you use a lined calligraphy pad, don't tear the pages out. Keep most of your work inside the pad. That way you'll have most of your work in one place.

If you have large, loose papers, consider buying an inexpensive cardboard portfolio to keep them in. You can find one at any art store. And, cardboard portfolios actually work better than the expensive leather portfolios!

Try Something New!

The activities in this book are just a few examples of fun calligraphy projects you can do. Once you've completed them all, check out some other kinds of Western calligraphy. You can also create your own styles of lettering. What kinds of writing are beautiful to you?

Other Styles of Calligraphy

- rustic capitals
- Roman square capitals
- uncial script
- Carolingian script
- Visigothic script
- antiqua script
- English script

30

GLOSSARY

confidence – a feeling of faith in your own abilities.

Gothic – of or related to the Gothic style of art or decoration. In particular, having the characteristics of a style of architecture popular in western Europe in the 12th through 16th centuries. The style emphasized pointed arches, vertical lines, and height.

horizontal – in the same direction as, or parallel to, the ground.

italic – a style of writing in which the letters slant upward to the right.

medieval – of or belonging to the Middle Ages, a period of time from AD 500 to 1500.

nib – the tip of a pen.

Roman Empire – the empire of ancient Rome, extending from Britain to North Africa to the Persian Gulf. Emperor Augustus began the empire in 27 BC. It lasted until AD 395, when it split into the Eastern and Western Roman Empires.

technique – a method or style in which something is done.

traditional – based on a usual or customary behavior, thought, style, or action passed from one generation to the next.

vertical – at a right angle, or perpendicular, to the ground.

Web Sites

To learn more about cool art, visit ABDO Publishing Company on the World Wide Web at **www.abdopublishing.com**. Web sites about cool art are featured on our Book Links page. These links are routinely monitored and updated to provide the most current information available.

INDEX